Swimming the Light

A Brief History of the Boston Light Swim

1976-2014

By Robert L. McCormack

Dedication

Special thanks are due the many Boston Light Swim Race volunteers, and also the boat people who accompany the swimmers along the course. They have done a remarkable job over the years. Without all of these dedicated people, it would not be possible to carry on this great tradition.

Congratulations to any swimmer who has ever even attempted the Boston Light Swim, including those who have finished the grind and those who have not. Because the success of the swim largely depends upon the conditions on that particular day, many who have failed to reach the finish line on one day may well have reached it on another. Hooray to all of you who have attempted the swim. You have had the courage to follow your aspirations and are thus all true winners.

It is to all of the volunteers, boat people, and every person who has ever attempted to swim the Boston Light, that this book is dedicated.

Boston Light in 1906
Credit Metropolitan News Company, Boston

Table of Contents

Introduction 1

Jim Doty 3

The Light by the Numbers 4

The Swims 6

Special Tributes 41

Sub-3-hour Swimmers of the 8-mile Boston Light Course .. 47

Two-way Swimmers 48

Kim Garbarino 48

Race Coordinators-1976-2014 49

About the Author 50

Introduction

Boston Light is located on Little *Brewster* Island in the outer Boston Harbor, about ten miles east of mainland Boston. By the late nineteenth century, many people had traveled from Boston to the Light by boat and it was natural that some of the more audacious would wonder whether such an enormous passage could be crossed by swimming. Several did actually attempt to swim from mainland Boston to the Light. Although some claimed to have successfully finished the swim, there is no documented evidence that any actually did make it. Interest, however, became so considerable that in 1907, the L Street Swimming Club, in South Boston, organized an official swim race.

There were no finishers in the first organized Boston Light Swim Race, held on July 29, 1907. Twenty-seven swimmers entered the water at the Charlestown Bridge for the twelve-mile swim and only three of the original 27 made it as far as George's Island, about two miles from the Light. By that point, the tide had changed direction and after 4 hours, 45 minutes, the three swimmers were taken from the water, unable to make headway against the current.

There was no organized race in 1908 although several people tried and failed to make the swim. In 1909 five individuals attempted six swims before the official race, but not one reached Boston Light. In the L Street Swimming Club's official race, held on August 29, one swimmer finally succeeded in reaching the goal. Austrian-born New York resident, Alois Anderle, age 40, finished the swim in 5 hours, 40 minutes. Despite being disqualified from the official race on a technicality when his hands inadvertently touched the sea bottom in the shallow shoal at Nix's Mate, Anderle is generally recognized as the first swimmer to ever succeed in the twelve-mile route from Chrlestown to Boston Light.

The following year, on August 7, 1910, 15-year-old Rose Pitonof of Dorchester, became the second swimmer, and first woman, to complete the swim. She was the only finisher in a field of twenty-one, with a time of 6 hours, 50 minutes. This women's record would hold up until 1926, when Mae Elwell broke it with a swim of 6 hours, 14 minutes.

The Boston Light Swim Race continued nearly every year through 1917, when a hiatus was observed due to the United States' entry into World War 1. The swim was resumed in 1921 and then held most years up through 1941. The course changed from time to time, and was eventually reduced to eight miles for safety reasons. The suspension was supposed to last only for the duration of the war but the official race would not be restarted for 35 long years.

The L Street Swimming Club

The L Street Baths go back to 1866 when the first bathhouse, a 2 ½ story building was built. That building was torn down in 1926 and a new one built in 1931 by Mayor James Michael Curley. The L Street Swimming Club was founded in 1905, to organize activities at the bathhouse, such as swimming races and picnics. The most famous of the club's activities in those pre-war days was the Charlestown to Boston Light Swim.

The L Street Brownies, members of the L Street baths, established themselves as a unified group in 1902. They organized the first New Year's Day Swim at L Street in 1904. The annual tradition continues to the present day.

Informal winter swims in South Boston actually had originated toward the latter years of the 19th century. The practice of cold-water bathing was probably started by immigrants who had swum in frigid conditions in their original countries, feeling that this was the way to good health and an active immune system. Over the century plus since then, there has never been a shortage of men, and, in modern times, women (the women swam at the "Girls L", the beach and bathhouse adjacent to the L Street beach), ready and willing to daily dive into the ice and snow-bound waters of Dorchester Bay.

Early L Street cold water swimmers
Credit: public domain

In 1955, 100-year-old L Street Brownie, Jacob Goldfarb's secret to longevity: "Swimming and girls." He may have been on to something. He lived until age 104.

Jim Doty

In the summer of 1968, 31-year-old James Jackson (Jim) Doty of Dedham came onto the Boston area ocean swimming scene. That year, he learned about the old Boston Light swim from a veteran Light swimmer, 58-year-old Bill Handley of Brighton. On September 15, Jim and Bill hired boats and went out to the Boston Light. Both men dove in at the Light but Bill decided to re-enter his boat after a mile or two. Jim swam on, arriving at South Boston Yacht Club, eight miles, and 4 hours, 32 minutes, later. Doty was hooked. Over the next 22 years he would complete a record sixteen solo swims of the Boston Light. In 1969, he swam the course round-trip, non-stop, a total of 16-miles. This was the first time a two-way swim had been accomplished over the 8-mile course, and Jim's established mark was 9 hours, 12 minutes. He left the dock at the yacht club at 7:36 a.m., reached the Light about noon, and then arrived back at the yacht club at 4:48 p.m. The seas were calm, with water temperature at 62 degrees. The two-way swim over the original 12-mile route, from Charlestown to Boston Light, for a total of 24 miles, had been accomplished three times previously:

Jim Doty
Credit Jim Doty

Sam Richards, 38, South Boston,
13 hours, 9 minutes, 1913

Charlie Toth, 35, South Boston,
15 hours, 27 minutes, 1915

Charlotte Arne, 17, Medford, 13 hours, 30 minutes, 1934

In 1976, Jim Doty ended the event's 35-year hiatus and reorganized the old Boston Light Swim Race. On August 14, six swimmers started at Boston Light bound for the Aquarium in Boston, a distance of about eleven miles. Three of the six swimmers finished, with the three others dropping out along the way. Fittingly, none other than Jim Doty won this first race of the modern era in a time of 5 hours, 39 minutes.

Girl Swims to Boston Light
IN SURPRISE SWIM TO LIGHT

A few days prior to Jim's 2-way attempt, he received a good luck phone call from Mrs. Charlotte Leverone, formerly Charlotte Arne.

The Light by the Numbers

In the 39 years between 1976 and 2014, there were 37 Boston Light Swim Races.

Distance (miles)	Number of swims
8	31
11	3
9*	1
6*	1
7*	1

* Shortened courses due to weather conditions

For the first three years, the course was 11 miles, from Boston Light to the New England Aquarium. In 1980, it was decided that the route up the Inner Harbor Channel to the Aquarium was too busy and, consequently, too dangerous. The course was changed to start from the Light and finish at the L Street Beach in South Boston, a distance of 8 miles.

In those 37 races, there were 436 starters and 322 finishers, for a total finishing rate of 74%.

By contrast, in the years from 1907 through 1941, 34 official Boston Light Swim Races were held:

Distance (miles)	Number of swims
12	22
8	11
6*	1

* Shortened courses due to weather conditions

In the 12-mile swims of the early era, there was a total of 264 starters and 35 finishers, or a finishing rate of 13%. In the eight-mile swims (including the one six-mile swim), there were 153 starters and 35 finishers, or a finishing rate of 23%. For the combined twelve and eight-mile swims, there were 417 starters and 70 finishers, or a total finishing rate of 17%.

Even considering the fact that many of the swims of the old era were twelve miles long, the difference in the finishing rate is startling, and the gap continues to widen. In the 20 races between 1976 and 1996, 65% of the starters finished the swim. In the 17 swims between 1998 and 2014, 80% of the starters finished.

Not only are a higher percentage of today's swimmers finishing the Boston Light Swim Race, the times are better. Of the 35 finishers in the 8-mile swims of the old era, only one swimmer finished in less than three hours, a rate of only 3%. In the modern era, of the 296 finishers of the 8-mile swim, 27 have finished in less than three hours, a rate of over 9%, a 200% improvement.

What accounts for the difference? There are many possibilities, including: training practices and swimming styles have evolved; more readily available coaching, both in the water and on-line; greater knowledge of the beneficial utilization of tides and currents.

Significantly, there are many more participants in the Boston Light Swim Races today than in the first half of the modern period. In the 20 races between 1976 and 1996 there were a total of 171 participants, or an average of fewer than nine starters per race. In the 17 swims between 1998 and 2014, 265 contestants have started the races, or an average of nearly sixteen swimmers per race, an increase of 78%. Indeed, in recent years, practically as soon as entry applicants are invited, quotas fill up.

The number of participants in the Boston Light Swim Races of the present day, the higher percentage of finishers, and the faster times, are all indications of a healthy and growing event. These factors, together with the dedicated race coordinators and volunteers, bode well for the future of this remarkable and important tradition.

Annette Kellerman, famous swimmer, vaudeville and motion picture star, tried the 12-mile Boston Light Swim in 1908. She got within about a half-mile of the finish but the adverse tidal current in the Black Rock Channel forced her to give up.

Kellerman was one of the more colorful characters in Boston Light history. She was arrested for indecency on Revere Beach, in 1907, at the age of 21, for wearing a one-piece bathing suit while other ladies of the day wore dresses, underwear, corsets and stockings for beach attire. Her popularity, and the popularity of the one-piece bathing suit that she introduced, eventually led to a lucrative business in which she publicized and sold her own line of swimwear.

A native Australian, she lived with her husband, James R. Sullivan, in the United States for a time. She performed in several movies in the silent film era, and, always the trendsetter, was the first person to appear nude on screen, in the movie, *A Daughter of the Gods*, in 1916, at the age of 30. She also performed for many years in vaudeville, exhibiting water ballet and high diving. She died in Australia in 1975 at the age of 89.

The Swims

1976

Left to right-Starrett, Gorman, Doty, Saperstein, Gula, Zaehring (arm only)
Credit Jim Doty

On the morning of August 14, 1976, six swimmers left the shore of Little Brewster Island, site of the Boston Light, in the morning, and headed west toward the New England Aquarium, in the inner Boston Harbor, a distance of about eleven miles.

Swimmers in the inaugural race were: Jim Doty, 39, Dedham; Dr. Joel Saperstein, 38, Medford; Jack Starrett, 52, Natick; Craig Zaehring, 35, Boston; Nancy Gorman, 30, Canton; and Fred Gula, 26, Palmer.

When they left Boston Light at about 9 a.m. conditions were calm, and remained so for most of the race, with low chop in the water, and a favorable tide. When the leaders reached the main channel of the inner harbor, however, a severe storm broke out, with wind, pelting rain, lightning and very choppy water. Gula and Gorman had already dropped out. Zaehring, leading for six miles, but swimming without goggles, was forced into his boat after entering the main Boston channel, his eyes inflamed from the salt water. Only Doty, Saperstein and Starrett fought on.

Finishers

1. Jim Doty, 5 hours, 39 minutes
2. Dr. Joel Saperstein, 5 hours, 41 minutes
3. Jack Starrett, time unknown

Non-finishers

Craig Zaehring
Nancy Gorman
Fred Gula

The first Boston Light Swim Race in 35 years was in the books, fittingly won by none-other than the person who had restarted it, Jim Doty.

1977

Fourteen swimmers dove in at Boston Light on the morning of August 6, 1977, with the destination again eleven miles away, at the New England Aquarium. Conditions were nearly calm, with only a slight chop in 66-degree water, and clear skies. The wind was blowing 12-15 miles an hour from the northwest. By the time the competitors reached the inner harbor, nine had retired into their boats. Continuing on were RoAnn Costin, Jay Pandya, Jim Doty, Sharon Levine, and Robert Sondheim.

Levine and Sondheim dropped out near Commonwealth Pier, leaving the other three heading for the finish at the aquarium. Results as follows:

Finishers
1. RoAnn Costin, 24, Nahant, 5 hours, 25 minutes
2. Jay Pandya, 16, Needham, 5 hours, 29 minutes
3. Jim Doty, 40, Dedham, 6 hours, 10 minutes

Non-finishers
Dr. Sharon Levine, 27, Cambridge
Robert Sondheim, Brookline
Lynne Gustafson, 25, Charlestown
Dr. Joel Saperstein, 39, Medford
Jack Clifford, 33, South Boston
Suni Pandya, 11, Needham
Craig Zaehring, 30, Boston
Robin Graf, 20, Simsbury, Connecticut
William Wing, 38, Mattapan
Lance Arlander, 30, Salem
Robert McCormack, 39, Brockton

At the end of the swim, Jim Doty was quoted in the Boston Globe: "Why should it bother me that a woman won? After all, there are only two sexes. One of us had to win."

Joel Saperstein, with Jack Clifford in background, at the start of the 1977 Boston Light Swim
Credit Jim Doty

1978

The third modern Boston Light Swim Race, from Boston Light to the New England Aquarium, was held on September 10, 1978. Under the auspices of the L Street Swimming Club the prior two years, the 1978 swim was sponsored by the New England Marathon Swimming Association, Inc. (NEMSA), the organization started by Jim Doty to promote and organize ocean swims, and to encourage and oversee clean, unpolluted waters in New England. NEMSA officers for this inaugural year were: Jim Doty, president, Dr. Joel Saperstein, vice-president, and Viking Gustafson, secretary.

At 11 a.m., twelve swimmers took to the water at Boston Light for the 11-mile grind to the aquarium. Water temperature was about 60 degrees with a low chop. A light wind blew from the east, a direction that aided the swimmers, because, unlike the two previous years, it didn't produce head-on waves. The chop would increase later on, however, and, of the twelve starters, only four made it to the finish line:

Finishers	**Those making it past the Long Island Bridge**
Brian Hanley, 28, Cambridge, 4 hours, 51 minutes	Jay Lodie
John Mulkern, Milton, 5 hours, 7 minutes	Lynne Gustafson
Jim Doty, 41, Dedham, 5 hours, 34 minutes	Greenbaum
Joni Beemsterboer, 23, San Francisco, 5 hours, 48 minutes	William Wing
	Burt Freedman

Winner, Brian Hanley
Credit Jim Doty

Second Place, John Mulkern
Credit Jim Doty

Third Place, Jim Doty
Credit Jim Doty

Fourth Place, Joni Beemsterboer
Credit Jim Doty

1979

No evidence of an official Boston Light Swim Race could be found, but in September, Karen Hartley, 22, of Dorchester, and Brian Hanley, 29, Cambridge, 1978's Boston Light Swim winner, swam together from Boston Light to L Street, eight miles, finishing side by side in 4 hours, 15 minutes. Karen would try the English Channel swim in 1980.

1980

The Boston Light Swim Race of 1980 took place on September 14. The starting point was moved forward from the Light to George's Island because of the prediction of headwinds. The destination was again the New England Aquarium, about nine miles away.

Thirteen swimmers dove into 62-degree water for the start at 9 a.m.; six managed to finish:

Finishers
1. Brian Hanley, 30, Cambridge, 4 hours, 10 minutes
2. Maura Fitzpatrick, 16, Westwood, 4 hours, 35 minutes
3. Jim Doty, 43, Dedham, 4 hours, 45 minutes
4. Peter Jurzynski, 29, Springfield, 4 hours, 57 minutes
5. Jay Lodie, 25, Boston, 5 hours, 2 minutes
6. Robert Sondheim, Sharon, 5 hours, 8 minutes

Non-finishers
Joe Nicholson, Cambridge
Phil Hresko, Newton
Viking Gustafson, 28, Charlestown
Jan Childs, Brookline
Joseph Coplan, New Haven, CT
Sam Osaka, Charlestown
Hal Gabriel, Newton

Karen Hartley
Credit Jim Doty

On September 20, Karen Hartley, 23, pride of Dorchester's Neponset section, attempted to swim across the English Channel, from France to England. She had arrived overseas on August 20, but bad weather precluded her attempt for an entire month. Karen was forced to retire four hours, and twelve miles, into the swim because of inflamed shoulder muscles. She had been reluctant to give up the swim, feeling that she would disappoint her sponsors, as well as herself, but decided not to risk permanent injury to her shoulders and possibly never be able to swim again. Six other swimmers made the attempt on the same day as Karen, but, through thunder and lightning storms, no one was able to finish.

1981

1981's Boston Light Swim was scheduled for Saturday, September 19, but due to fog and rain it was postponed until the following day. Because of the continuing threat of high winds, fog and rain on that day, the swim started at George's Island, with the destination about six miles away at the L Street Beach. The weather turned out better than expected but the seas were still choppy, with waves at two-feet. Six swimmers persevered to the finish.

1. Todd Bryan, Rhode Island, 2 hours, 38 minutes
2. Sharon Beckman, 23, Illinois, 2 hours, 51 minutes
3. Karen Hartley, 24, Dorchester, 3 hours, 10 minutes
4. Bill Cosgrove, Dorchester, 3 hours, 33 minutes
5. Stan Luniewicz, 28, Dorchester, 3 hours, 40 minutes
6. Jim Doty, 44, Dedham, 3 hours, 43 minutes

1982

On Saturday, September 11, ten swimmers entered 61-degree water at Boston Light for the eight-mile swim to L Street. Conditions were ideal, with light winds and warm air temperature. Nine of the ten starters stayed in to the finish.

Finishers
1. Sharon Beckman, 24, Cambridge, 3 hours, 7 minutes
2. Margie Cassidy, 21, Wilmington, DE, 3 hours, 12 minutes
3. Karen Hartley, 25, Dorchester, 3 hours, 19 minutes
4. Brian Hanley, 32, Cambridge, 3 hours, 30 minutes
5. Bill Dineen, Lynnfield, 3 hours, 36 minutes
6. Bill Cosgrove, Dorchester, 3 hours, 58 minutes
7. Jim Doty, 45, Dedham, 4 hours, 9 minutes
8. Fred Gula, 32, Monson, 4 hours, 14 minutes
9. Arthur Madore, Dorchester, 4 hours, 39 minutes

Non-finishers
Stan Luniewicz, 29, Dorchester

On August 28, Sharon Beckman, 24, of Cambridge, succeeded in swimming the English Channel, from England to France, in a time of 9 hours, 7 minutes. She became the first New England woman to ever accomplish the feat. She arrived in England on August 2, but weather and water conditions did not allow the swim until the 28th. She said that one of the biggest problems of the crossing was climbing over the rocks at the finish beach in France, at Cape Gris Nez, where she suffered cuts and bruises all over her body. Amazingly, Sharon returned from England and just two weeks later, entered and won the Boston Light Swim of 1982.

On September 14, Karen Hartley, 25, of Dorchester, swam the 28.5-mile Manhattan Island Marathon, finishing third in a field of twelve competitors, ten men and two women. Karen finished in front of the one other woman, and eight of the ten men, in a time of 7 hours, 37 minutes, setting the women's record for the swim. She beat the previous record of 7 hours, 57 minutes, set by Diana Nyad in 1975.

In the September 17, 1962 edition of the *Boston Herald,* Huck Finnegan reported on the 1925 Women's Boston Light Swim, which was won by 17-year-old Irene Hesenius, of Winthrop, in the second fastest women's time ever, 7 hours, 9 minutes. Huck said that Irene was not a distance swimmer, just swam for the fun of it at Winthrop Beach from a very early age.

She started the 1925 swim with no boat pilot. Famous Boston Light swimmer, Sam Richards, joined her in his boat two miles from the start. Sam had been piloting Eva Morrison but, off Governor's Island, quit her after an argument about what was the correct course. He then switched to Hesenius. "I wouldn't have made it without Sam", Irene said. "Frankly, I didn't know how far away Boston Light was. Nor did I know the importance of the tides. Mayor Curley presented me with a trophy and when he got a look at me he said, 'Any little girl who wins such a big race deserves a bigger trophy than this', and, by golly, he got a bigger one for me."

On New Year's Day, 1926, Irene Hesenius broke the ice at Orient Heights Yacht Club for the New Year's Day annual dip. It was that same year that Gertrude Ederle became the first woman to successfully swim the English Channel. Irene Hesenius briefly entertained the thought of making the attempt herself, but instead eloped with a young man named Morris. "No regrets," she said.

Irene passed away on November 8, 2002, at the age of 94.

Irene Hesenius in Winter at Orient Heights
Credit Boston Public Library-Leslie Jones Collection

1983

1983's Boston Light Swim Race was held on September 10. Fourteen swimmers left the Light at 9 a.m. bound for L Street, eight miles ahead. Wind was light from the West but picked up around 11 a.m. to about 15 miles per hour. Four of the fourteen swimmers retired along the way, but ten hung on to the finish.

1. Margaret Broenniman, 20, Smith College student, Washington, D.C., 3 hours, 27 minutes
2. Maura Fitzpatrick, 19, Smith College student, Westwood, 3 hours, 43 minutes
3. Jeff Sheard, 32, Columbus, Ohio, 3 hours, 51 minutes
4. Peter Jurzynski, 32, Stoneham, 3 hours, 52 minutes
5. Regina Armstrong, New Jersey, 4 hours, 1 minute
6. Dale Petranech, New Jersey, 4 hours, 6 minutes
7. Bill Dineen, Lynnfield, 4 hours, 17 minutes
8. Jim Doty, 46, Dedham, 4 hours, 32 minutes
9. Joel Saperstein, 45, Medford, 4 hours, 34 minutes
10. Ed Keegan, West Roxbury, 4 hours, 48 minutes

Non-finishers
Arthur Madore, Dorchester
Kathy Loomis, New York
Ralph Willard, 69, Peekskill, New York
Stan Lunewicz, 30, Dorchester

On July 24, Karen Hartley, now 26, of Dorchester swam the 28.5 miles around Manhattan Island, New York, finishing fifteenth in a field of twenty-one swimmers. This was the second time she finished this swim, coming ashore in 9 hours.

On April 4, 1983, great two-way Boston Light Swimmer, Charlotte Arne-Leverone, of Arlington, died, after suffering a stroke, at age 66. Charlotte was the third person, and first and only woman, to swim from Charlestown to Boston Light and back, a total distance of 24 miles. She accomplished this great feat, at the age of 17, on September 3, 1934, in a time of 13 hours, 30 minutes. Her time was second to that of Sam Richards, who swam a round-trip in 1913 in 13 hours, 9 minutes.

1984

On September 1, 1984, thirteen swimmers dove into 61-degree water at Boston Light and began the eight mile swim for the L Street Beach. Some time after the start, the wind increased to 20 miles per hour, and the water kicked up into a high chop, especially after the Long Island Bridge. Only three swimmers eventually succeeded in finishing, with ten dropping out of the very choppy water along the way.

Finishers

1. Jeff Sheard, 33, Columbus, Ohio, 3 hours, 41 minutes
2. Peter Jurzynski, 33, South Boston, 4 hours, 17 minutes
3. Jim Doty, 47, Dedham, 5 hours, 15 minutes

Non-finishers

Ed Keegan, West Roxbury, 4 hours, 15 minutes

Kathy Loomis, New York, New York, 4 hours, 31 minutes

John Murray, Charlestown, 4 hours, 5 minutes

Bill Cosgrove, South Boston, 3 hours, 50 minutes

Stan Luniewicz, 31, Dorchester, 3 hours, 45 minutes

Roger Little, Bedford, 3 hours, 40 minutes

Ralph Willard, 70, Peekskill, New York, 3 hours, 15 minutes

Bill Dineen, Lynnfield, 3 hours, 5 minutes

Dr. John Schrum, Charlottesville, Virginia, 1 hour, 15 minutes

Dick Henlotter, Swampscott, 1 hour, 10 minutes

On August 18, two seniors at Smith College succeeded in swimming the English Channel: Maura Fitzpatrick, 20, of Westwood, second finisher of the Boston Light Swims of 1980 and 1983; and Margaret Broenniman, 21, of Chevy Chase, Maryland, winner of the Boston Light Swim of 1983. They took to the water together at Shakespeare Beach, Dover, England, at 4:55 a.m. At about 4:20 p.m. both women waded ashore, within ten minutes of each other, at Cape Gris-Nez, France, in a time of about 11 ½ hours.

On June 15, 1984, the great Rose Pitonof-Weene passed away at the age of 89. Rose, a native of Dorchester, was the second successful finisher, and very first woman, of the 12-mile Boston Light Swim, in 1910, at the tender age of 15. Her time, 6 hours, 50 minutes, was the women's record for the swim until broken by Mae Elwell, of Revere, in 1926. She also completed a swim to Graves Light from Charlestown, 12 miles, on August 17, 1914, in 6 hours, 21 minutes, becoming the first woman to do so. Rose left a gigantic legacy of long-distance swimming prowess, in Boston and around the country.

Rose Pitonof
Credit *Boston Journal*, August 2, 1910

1985

On September 7, at 11 a.m., ten solo swimmers and two relay teams, left the Boston Light in 63-degree water, on the eight mile swim to the L Street Beach (1985 marked the first year in which relay teams were included. A relay team could consist of any number of swimmers, and required at least one swimmer to be in the water from the beginning of the swim to the end). It was very windy that morning, from the northeast, but gradually it died down until conditions became nearly ideal, with low wind and chop and sunny skies. Nine of the ten swimmers finished as follows:

1. Nathalie Patenaude, Quebec, Canada, 3 hours, 8 minutes
2. Jeff Sheard, 34, Columbus, Ohio, 3 hours, 9 minutes
3. Tony Young, Bethesda, Maryland, 3 hours, 29 minutes
4. Peter Jurzynski, 34, South Boston, 3 hours, 40 minutes
5. Bob Lazzaro, Belmont, 3 hours, 40 minutes (33 seconds after Jurzynski)
6. Dr. Herb Barthels, Santa Barbara, California, 3 hours, 51 minutes
7. Jim Doty, 48, Dedham, 4 hours, 32 minutes
8. Tom Carmody, Lynn, 4 hours, 47 minutes,
9. Peter Gallagher, South Boston, 4 hours, 49 minutes

Kathy Loomis, New York, New York, did not finish

Relay Teams
1. Hennessey, Macher, Spencer and Muise, 3 hours, 21 minutes
2. Murray, McCormick, Cochran, 3 hours, 21 minutes (14 seconds later)

On July 28, just over a month prior to his second place finish in the 1985 Boston Light Swim, Jeff Sheard completed the 28.5 mile Manhattan Island Marathon Swim, finishing eighth in a time of 8 hours, 16 minutes.

On March 17, 1985, Eva Morrison Abdou, famous Boston Light swimmer, died in Brockton, after a long illness. The obituary reports Eva's age as 72 but swimming archives indicate that she was 80. Her first Boston Light swim was in 1924, at the age of 19, and she went on to finish at least five more. Her 1924 swim marked her as the fourth woman to ever finish the swim. All of her Boston Light swims were over the 12-mile route. She also completed the 12-mile swim from Charlestown to Graves Light in 1931. She made three attempts at the English Channel, in 1924, 1935 and 1937, but was defeated each time by severe weather and water conditions. She was born in Pictou, Nova Scotia but moved at an early age to Revere. At the time of her passing she was a resident of Scituate.

Eva Morrison in 1924
Credit Library of Congress,
LC-B2200-11

1986

Eight solo swimmers and one relay team member left the Light at 12:45 p.m. on September 13. They had to buck a 20 mile per hour headwind. Water temperature stayed at about 60 degrees. The cold water forced three swimmers, John Schrum, George MacMasters and Fran Fidler, out. Jim Doty retired because of an ulcer attack near the Long Island Bridge. Four swimmers reached the L Street Beach.

Marcy MacDonald and family after the swim
Credit the MacDonald family

Finishers

1. Marcy MacDonald, 22, Manchester, Connecticut, 4 hours, 4 minutes
2. Jeff Sheard, 35, Columbus, Ohio, 4 hours, 11 minutes
3. Peter Jurzynski, 35, South Boston, 4 hours, 30 minutes
4. Karen Hartley, 29, Dorchester, 5 hours, 33 minutes

Non-finishers

John Schrum
Jim Doty
George MacMasters
Fran Fidler

Relay Team

Tom Hyde, Tom Walsh, Paula Toomey, Jim McHugh, 5 hours, 40 minutes

Peter Jurzynski's Great English Channel Record

Date	Time	Age
August, 1987	12 hours, 7 minutes	36
August, 1988	13 hours, 21 minutes	37
August, 1992	13 hours, 20 minutes	41
July, 1996	13 hours, 40 minutes	45
July, 1997	13 hours, 49 minutes	46
August, 1998	16 hours, 16 minutes	47
July, 1999	14 hours, 57 minutes	48
July, 2000	14 hours, 5 minutes	49
July, 2002	17 hours, 8 minutes	51
August, 2003	14 hours, 57 minutes	52
July, 2004	17 hours, 18 minutes	53
July, 2005	15 hours, 30 minutes	54
July, 2006	16 hours, 43 minutes	55
August, 2007	16 hours, 21 minutes	56

One week before the Boston Light Swim, on September 6, Michael E. Glynn, a young swimmer from South Boston, was struck and killed by a motorboat towing a water skier in Boston Harbor, between L Street and Carson Beach. Mike was in training for the 1986 Boston Light Swim.

On July 30, just a month and a half before his Boston Light second place finish, Jeff Sheard swam across the English Channel, from England to France, in a time of 11 hours, 8 minutes.

On July 20, Karen Hartley, 29, of Dorchester, made her third attempt at the 28.5-mile Manhattan Island Marathon Swim (She had finished the swim in 1982 and 1983). The 1986 swim started, in 65-degree water, at 96th Street in the East River. The field consisted of 23 swimmers, 14 men and 9 women. Karen managed about 14 miles, in four hours, and then was forced out in choppy water, two miles south of the George Washington Bridge, in the Hudson River, with the same shoulder injury that had forced her into the boat during her English Channel attempt in 1980.

1987

This year's Boston Light Swim was held on September 5. It was named in honor of Michael E. Glynn, the swimmer who was killed by a boat the previous summer. The starting point was moved forward a mile or so, to the end of the Brewster Island Spit, due to a full moon that produced a higher than normal tide, and a late start. The "moon tide" made it impractical to start the race early because of the difficulty of swimming against the strong outgoing current. The course was thus shortened to about seven miles so that all of the swimmers could finish in daylight.

Ten contestants dove in at 1:45 p.m.: nine solo swimmers and one member of a team of three relay swimmers. Six of the solo swimmers and the relay team finished.

Finishers
1. Marcy MacDonald, 23, Manchester, Connecticut, 2 hours, 55 minutes
2. Paul Jagasich, Virginia, 3 hours, 15 minutes
3. Peter Jurzynski, 36, South Boston, 3 hours, 35 minutes
4. Karen Hartley, 30, Dorchester, 3 hours, 42 minutes
5. John Channell, Walpole, 3 hours, 57 minutes
6. Jim Doty, 50, Dedham, 4 hours, 12 minutes

Relay Team
MacMasters, Baxter and
Murnane, 3 hours, 45 minutes

Non-finishers
John Shrum
Paula Toomey
Fran Fidler

On August 4, Peter Jurzynski, made his first successful swim across the English Channel, from England to France. He had planned to make the effort in each of the prior two years, traveling to England both years, but bad conditions precluded the attempts. By the year 2007, Peter would go on to complete a total of 14 crossings, an American record until 2014. He stated at the time of his first successful crossing that if it had not been for the people of South Boston, he would not have been able to achieve the swimming of the channel. Most of Peter's training was at the L Street beach and bathhouse, in South Boston.

1988

Four solo swimmers and members of two four-person relay teams left Boston Light at noon on September 3. The water was 62 degrees and relatively flat at the start, but became choppy from the Long Island Bridge to L Street, due to the large number of pleasure boats in the area. All of the solo and relay swimmers succeeded in finishing the swim:

1. David Van Mouwerik, Acton, 3 hours, 14 minutes
2. Peter Jurzynski, 37, South Boston, 4 hours, 21 minutes
3. Gregg Thompson, Wilson, North Carolina, 4 hours, 23 minutes
4. Jim Doty, 51, Dedham, 4 hours, 33 minutes

Relay teams
1. Steve Puopolo, Richard Puopolo, Richard Fay and Lynn Murnane, 3 hours, 38 minutes
2. Stan Luniewicz, Tom Hyde, Steve Buckley and Carol Weston, 3 hours, 49 minutes

Third Place Finisher, Gregg Thompson
Credit Jim Doty

Second Place Finisher, Peter Jurzynski
Credit Jim Doty

On August 27, 1988, Boston Light and English Channel swimmer, Jeff Sheard, 37, of Columbus, Ohio, completed his second 28.5 mile Manhattan Island Marathon Swim, finishing ninth in a time of 8 hours, 5 minutes.

1989

On September 5, at 12:30 p.m., five solo swimmers and members of four relay teams dove in at Boston Light. Conditions included 63-degree water, a slight chop and bright sunshine. The water became choppier, and somewhat warmer on the Boston side of the Long Island Bridge. All five solo swimmers, and the fifteen relay swimmers, succeeded in reaching the L Street Beach.

Finishers
1. Jim Peters, Sudbury, 3 hours, 17 minutes
2. Debbie Druyff, Danbury, Connecticut, 3 hours, 30 minutes
3. George MacMasters, 32, Dorchester, 3 hours, 41 minutes
4. Richard Puopolo, East Boston, 4 hours, 43 minutes
5. Jim Doty, 52, Dedham, 4 hours, 47 minutes

Relay Teams
1. Richalie Cranmer, Maureen Ford, Ric Fay, Steve Puopolo, 3 hours, 43 minutes
2. Dan Cooke, Dave Cochrane, Paul Hennessey, Joe McDermott, 3 hours, 46 minutes
3. Stan Luniewicz, John Murray, Mike Ohrt, 3 hours, 47 minutes
4. Tom Hyde, Lynn Murnane, Paula Toomey, Bob Sullivan, 4 hours, 30 minutes

1990

1990's Boston Light swimmers left the Light in fog and 65 degree, choppy water. Seven of the eight solo swimmers and all of the three relay teams finished at L Street.

Finishers
1. Jim Peters, Sudbury, 3 hours, 30 minutes
2. Bill Cosgrove, Dorchester, 4 hours, 35 minutes
3. Richard Puopolo, East Boston, 4 hours, 49 minutes
4. Brian Holmes, 5 hours, 6 minutes
5. Jim Doty, 53, Dedham, 5 hours, 39 minutes
6. Paul Braun, 5 hours, 55 minutes
7. David Smith, 6 hours, 12 minutes

Steve Buckley did not finish; he reached Long Island Bridge

Relay Teams
1. Lynn Murnane, Bob Sullivan, Bill Paine, Richie Martin, 3 hours, 42 minutes
2. Stan Luniewicz, Mike Ohrt, John Murray, Bruce Hunter, 3 hours, 47 minutes
3. Paula Toomey, Steve Puopolo, Sarah Evans, Melinda Trotti, Carol Weston, 4 hours, 40 minutes

1991

August 17, 1991, at 11:15 a.m., five solo swimmers and three relay team members left Boston Light. All five solo swimmers, and the three relay teams, reached the L Street Beach:

1. William Paine, 3 hours, 41 minutes
2. George MacMasters, 34, Dorchester, 3 hours, 55 minutes
3. Richard Puopolo, East Boston, 4 hours, 5 minutes
4. Brian Holmes, 4 hours, 54 minutes
5. David Smith, 5 hours, 24 minutes

Relay teams:
1. Stan Luniewicz, Sharon Beckman, Mike Ohrt, 3 hours, 42 minutes
2. Lynn Murnane, Jones, Samuels, Bob Sullivan, 3 hours, 44 minutes
3. Paula Toomey, Steve Puopolo, Sarah Evans, 4 hours, 24 minutes

Records of the 1991 Boston Light Swim are unclear. The starters' list designates "Smith, Paine, Pinto, Puopolo, Post, Holmes and Doty," but the finishers' list mentions, "Paine, MacMasters, Puopolo, Holmes and Smith." There is no mention of non-finishers, if any. The author's opinion, in the absence of more complete evidence, is that only the above five soloists started and finished the swim.

Jerry Nason commented in his column in the Boston Globe of July 21, 1964 that Jack Starrett, age 39, of Natick, was training for an attempt at the English Channel in August. Jack had recently finished a 12-mile training swim from Cohasset to the Boston Light. Some days later he swam from Falmouth Heights to Martha's Vineyard in a fog, in a time of about four hours.

Jack, afflicted with cerebral palsy from birth, was going to try to be the third Massachusetts man (Boston Light swimmers, Henry Sullivan of Lowell and Charlie Toth of South Boston both made successful crossings in 1923.), and first with cerebral palsy, to succeed in the channel swim. On August 4, he did succeed in swimming across the English Channel, from Cape Gris Nez, France to Folkstone, England in a time of 12 hours, 45 minutes.

Associated Press photo 8/6/64

Jack went on to swim the 12 miles from Charlestown to Graves Light in 1972, and the Boston Light Swim, about 11 miles, from the Light to the New England Aquarium, in the first race of the modern era, 1976.

On September 23, 1991, Jack passed away at the age of 66. In addition to his English Channel, Boston Light and Graves Light swims, he swam across the Northumberland Strait, Canada. He also completed many difficult swims as a professional marathon swimmer for several years. He was a friend and mentor to many in the marathon swimming community and would be sorely missed.

1992

1992's Boston Light Swim got off on Sunday, August 30, after a one-day delay due to stormy weather. The weather on the 30th was still windy and the water very choppy. Six solo swimmers, and three relay team members left the light in the morning. So severe were the conditions that only three of the six solo swimmers reached L Street, while all three relay teams managed to finish.

Finishers
1. Bob Bristow, 3 hours, 4 minutes
2. George MacMasters, 35, Dorchester, 3 hours, 19 minutes
3. Mike Welsch, 33, Ware, Massachusetts, 5 hours, 38 minutes

Relay teams
1. Clare Powers, William Paine, Richie Martin, 3 hours, 23 minutes
2. Stan Luniewicz, Stephen Harris, Bill Dineen, Jim Doty, 3 hours, 53 minutes
3. Lynn Murnane, Tom Hyde, Bob Sullivan, David Smith, 5 hours, 19 minutes

Non-finishers
Steve Buckley
Julie Burnett

Mike Welsch (Iron Mike) was a Dorchester native who had lost a leg in a motorcycle accident at age 20. He hung on and finished the Boston Light Swim in very rough conditions. Mike had completed the eleven-mile Egg Rock Swim in Nahant a month prior to the Light Swim, in a time of 5 hours, 15 minutes, also in rough conditions.

1993

August 21 was the date of the Boston Light Swim of 1993. The swimmers left the Light at 8:45 a.m.

Finishers
1. Julie Burnett, 27, Stoneham, 3 hours 41 minutes
2. Dan Dellucka, 4 hours, 13 minutes
3. Mike Welsch (Iron Mike did it again), 34, Burlington, 4 hours, 27 minutes

Relay teams
1. Stan Luniewicz, Bill Dineen, Bruce Hunter, 3 hours, 54 minutes
2. Bob Sullivan, Jim Doty, Peter Gallagher, Bill Silvestri, 4 hours, 16 minutes

1994

1994's Boston Light Swim went off at 10 a.m. on August 27. Seven solo swimmers and three relay team members left the Light at 10 a.m. The water was about 66 degrees, with a low chop. It grew choppier and warmer past the Long Island Bridge. Four of the solo swimmers, and all of the relay teams finished at L Street:

Finishers
1. Julie Burnett, 28, Stoneham, 3 hours, 38 minutes
2. Richie Martin, Gloucester, 4 hours, 2 minutes
3. John Canniff, 37, Roslindale, 4 hours, 32 minutes
4. Mike Welsch (Iron Mike did it for the third time), 35, Burlington, 4 hours, 51 minutes

Relay Teams
1. Wendy James, Scott Winslow, Tom Hotaling, Shari Hersh, 3 hours 20 minutes
2. Stan Luniewicz, Tim Connolly, Damon Burchard, 4 hours, 40 minutes
3. Bob Sullivan, Roberta Allison, Bill Sylvestri, Jim Doty, 4 hours, 59 minutes

Non-finishers
John O'Connell
John Tom
John Post

Jim Doty finishing Boston Light Swim-mid 1990s
Credit Jim Doty family

On August 15, 37-year-old Dorchester swimmer, George MacMasters, swam across the English Channel, from Shakespeare Beach, Dover, England, to Le Petit Blanc-Nez, France, in a time of 12 hours, 10 minutes. George was very well known in the ocean swimming community around Boston, having completed three Boston Light Swims, and the 11-mile Egg Rock Swim in Nahant. This was George's second try at the Channel. He failed to complete it in 1993.

Joseph (Jay) Lodie, accomplished ocean swimmer, and friend to many in and around the Boston ocean waters, passed away on January 9, 1994, after a lengthy illness. Jay was 38 years of age. He had successfully swum the Boston Light Swim Race in 1980.

Dr. Marcy MacDonald, 30, of Andover, Connecticut, winner of the Boston Light Swims in 1986 and 1987, successfully swam across the English Channel on June 30.

On September 10, Boston Light swimmer, Julie Burnett, 28, of Stoneham, was part of a six-member women's relay team that set a new record in the 28.5 mile Manhattan Island Marathon Swim- 6 hours, 20 minutes. The old record was 7 hours, 14 minutes.

Amazingly, Julie had finished the same marathon swim solo just three weeks before, on August 20, finishing eighth in a time of 7 hours, 57 minutes. She would go on to make the swim again in 1995, finishing fourth in 8 hours, 24 minutes, and again in a relay in 1998, finishing in third place in a time of 7 hours, 50 minutes.

On July 29, Marcia Cleveland of Illinois swam across the English Channel in a time of 9 hours, 44 minutes. Marcia would swim Boston Light in 2002.

1995

The 1995 Boston Light Swim started from the Light at 6:15 a.m. on August 26. Ten solo swimmers and six relay teams participated. The conditions were ideal, with flat, 68 degree water, and sunny skies. Results as follows:

1. David Alleva, 41, Quincy, 2 hours, 20 minutes
2. Kasim Kazbay, 32, New York, 2 hours, 49 minutes
3. Art Lutschaunig, Boston, 2 hours, 50 minutes
4. Marcy MacDonald, 31, Andover, Connecticut, 2 hours, 59 minutes
5. Tom O'Brien, South Boston, 3 hours, 22 minutes
6. Tom Dugan, 44, Norton, 3 hours 28 minutes
7. Mike Welsch (Iron Mike did it for the fourth time), 36, Woburn, 3 hours, 34 minutes
8. Richard Kanosky, 34, Marblehead, 5 hours, 45 minutes
9. Dr. Selwyn Kanosky, 66, Marblehead, 5 hours, 45 minutes

Julie Burnett, the previous year's winner, was forced to retire after the Long Island Bridge because of a pulled muscle in her shoulder.

Relay Teams
1. Gutierrez, Powers, Sumbera, Hirst, 2 hours, 46 minutes
2. Martin, Lowrey, Berry, Swensen, 2 hours, 48 minutes
3. Luniewicz, Ohrt, Hunter, Pandya, 3 hours, 13 minutes
4. Connolly, Gallery, Fisher, 3 hours, 28 minutes
5. Sullivan, Doty, Silvestri, Rome, Weston, 3 hours, 34 minutes
6. Roberta Allison, Don Allison, Alesse, Ghirdon, 4 hours, 18 minutes

Two records were set during this year's swim: David Alleva set a new record for men's time. The previous record of 2 hours, 46 minutes was set in 1940 by Billy Nolan of Charlestown.

Dr. Selwyn Kanosky, age 66, paced by his son, Richard, set a record as the oldest finisher in the history of the Boston Light Swim to date. Dr. Kanosky was a cardiologist in Marblehead. He passed away on July 11, 2010. His obituary in the Salem News. states that he was "an avid swimmer and at one time saved the lives of two drowning men." Unfortunately, his son, Richard, who swam with his dad in the Boston Light Swim of 1995, predeceased Selwyn, on April 7, 2002, at the age of 41.

Boston marathon swim legend, Jim Doty announced his retirement as Clerk of Course after the Boston Light Swim Race of 1995. He continued to participate for several more years, as race advisor and volunteer.

Boston Light swimmer, Julie Burnett, 29, of Stoneham, became the first woman to swim the length of Lake Winnipesaukee in New Hampshire. Her time for the 22-mile grind was 11 hours, 3 minutes. Julie started at Downing's Marina in Alton, and finished at Center Harbor.

1996

1996's Boston Light Swim began at the Light at 8:30 a.m. on August 17. The torch for this year's race organization had passed from Jim Doty to Andrew Frackiewicz as Clerk of Course.

Finishers
1. David Alleva, 42, Quincy, 2 hours, 23 minutes
   (second to his own all-time record time of 2 hours, 20 minutes, set in 1995)
2. John O'Connell, Quincy, 2 hours, 40 minutes (third fastest all-time to date, beating Billy Nolan of Charlestown's 1940 record of 2 hours 46 minutes. Nolan is now in fourth place all-time)
3. Kathleen Hines, New York, 2 hours, 54 minutes
4. John Langton, 29, Woburn, 2 hours, 58 minutes
5. Jennifer Dutton, 27, Natick, 3 hours, 2 minutes
6. Tom Dugan, 45, Brockton, 3 hours, 14 minutes
7. John Canniff, Roslindale, 3 hours, 19 minutes
8. Ann Marie D'Agostino, Boston, 3 hours, 21 minutes

1997

This year's Boston Light Swim was scheduled for August 23, but the writer could find no record of the swim having taken place.

1998

Seven swimmers out of fourteen starters finished the swim. One wetsuit swimmer also finished, but, in accordance with Boston Light Swim Race rules, a swimmer wearing a wetsuit does not get credit for finishing the swim.

Finishers

1. Irena Sumbera, Orleans, 3 hours, 13 minutes
2. John Langton, 31, Woburn, 3 hours, 24 minutes
3. Jennifer Dutton, 29, Natick, 3 hours, 43 minutes
4. Eileen Burke, 35, 3 hours, 49 minutes
5. Tom Dugan, 47, Brockton, 4 hours, 4 minutes
6. John Werner, 28, Dorchester, 4 hours, 32 minutes
7. Debra Taylor, 6 hours

Relay Teams

1. Lazzaro, etc., 2 hours, 58 minutes
2. Connolly, etc., 3 hours, 18 minutes
3. Campbell, etc., 3 hours, 39 minutes
4. Doty, etc., 4 hours, 25 minutes

Kate Matwychuk, 27, (wetsuit), Ontario, Canada, 3 hours, 23 minutes

Non-finishers

George Wallace

Nancy Monbouquette

Jeremy Grosvenor

Jim McSherry

Sandy Rapkin

John Canniff

Fred Gula

Race Coordinator Andy Frackiewicz

1999

The Boston Light Swim of 1999 started at 8 a.m. on August 14. The water was a choppy 60 degrees. It was pouring rain. The torch was passed from Andy Frackiewicz to John Werner, who served as race coordinator. Results as follows:

1. Tom Dugan, 48, Norton, 4 hours, 36 minutes
2. John Werner, 29, Dorchester, 4 hours, 57 minutes
3. James McHugh, 43, Watertown, 5 hours, 42 minutes
4. Jennifer Dutton, 30, Framingham, time not recorded (tnr)
5. Anne Marie D'Agostino, tnr
6. Nancy Monbouquette, tnr

Relay Teams

1. Fred Schlicher, Coe Schlicher, Will Ridell, tnr
2. Jim Doty, Bob Sullivan, Bill Silvestri, Lou Murray, tnr

2000

The Boston Light Swim for 2000 started at the Light at 8:23 a.m. on August 12. Rough seas delayed the start by 23 minutes. The wind was blowing strongly, some estimates say 30 miles per hour, creating substantial wave action. It was a following sea at the start but changed to approaching from the right side after the Long Island Bridge. Water temperature was about 65 degrees.

Thirteen solo swimmers started the swim but, within an hour or so, four contestants retired. Nine swimmers fought the battle to the end, all landing at L Street Beach as follows:

1. Meryem Tangoren-Masood, New York, 3 hours, 31 minutes
2. Fred Schlicher, 50, Medford, 3 hours, 31 minutes (29 seconds behind first place)
3. Irena Sumbera, Orleans, 3 hours, 41 minutes
4. Fred Knight, 50, Wayland, 3 hours, 58 minutes
5. Rex Painter, St. Augustine, Florida, 3 hours, 59 minutes
6. John Langton, 33, Somerville, 4 hours, 33 minutes
   Anne Marie D'Agostino, Boston, 4 hours, 33 minutes (tied with Langton)
   Julie Burnett, 34, Stoneham, 4 hours, 33 minutes (tied with Langton and D'Agostino)
9. John Werner, 30, Dorchester, 5 hours, 44 minutes

Non-finishers

George Wallace

Tom Dugan

Two other swimmers (names not recorded)

Race coordinator, John Werner.

2001

The 2001 Boston Light Swim started three hours before high tide, at 8:05 a.m. on August 18. This would result in an out-going (adverse) current for the last part of the race. The water was a choppy 58 degrees at the start, wind from the southeast. Conditions were rough throughout the entire race, but especially so after the Long Island Bridge, when the following sea changed to waves from the right side. The wind and chop grew worse for the last mile and a half, along the stretch from Thompson Island to L Street.

Of the fourteen solo starters, five hung on to the finish at L Street. One wetsuit swimmer also finished, but, again, in accordance with Boston Light Swim Race rules, a swimmer wearing a wetsuit does not get credit for finishing the swim. Both relay teams also arrived at the finish line.

1. Fred Knight, 51, Wayland, 4 hours, 59 minutes
2. Victor Maldonado, 37, Watertown, 5 hours, 3 minutes
3. Nat Mason, West Chatham, 5 hours, 24 minutes

4. Jennifer Dutton, 32, Framingham, 6 hours, 7 minutes
5. Michael Welsch (Iron Mike's fifth successful swim), 42, Woburn, 7 hours, 28 minutes

Jeremiah Fitzgibbons (wetsuit), 4 hours, 7 minutes

Relay Teams

1. Joe Sheehan, Kenneth Lawler, David Swensen, 2 hours, 56 minutes
2. John Langton, Jr., Julie Burnett, Tom Dugan, 6 hours, 34 minutes

Because of the very rough conditions, and the extreme difficulty of bucking the outgoing tide getting around Thompson Island, race coordinator, John Werner, declared a second (concurrent) race, from Boston Light to Thompson Island, with finishers as follows:

1. Jim McSherry, Woburn, 5 hours, 43 minutes
2. John Werner, 31, Dorchester, 5 hours, 55 minutes
3. William Chrisman, Paradise Valley, 8 hours, 12 minutes

Race coordinator, John Werner.

2002

The Boston Light Swim Race for 2002 started at 7:30 a.m. on August 24. The previous year's mistake of starting only three hours before high tide was not repeated. Swimmers dove in about five and a half hours before high tide, therefore they were assisted by a tidal push throughout the entire swim. Water temperature at the Light was 62 degrees, and rose to 65 from the Long Island Bridge to L Street. Twelve solo swimmers and two relay team members jumped in at the Light. Wind was about 10 miles per hour, with water at a slight chop. After the Long Island Bridge, and into the open water before Spectacle Island, the chop got much tougher. Despite the challenge of the choppy sea, eleven of the twelve solo swimmers, and both of the relay teams, managed to reach L Street.

Finishers

1. Marcia Cleveland, 38, Riverside, Connecticut, 2 hours, 47 minutes
2. Nicholas Sidelnik, 20, Overland Park, Kansas, 2 hours, 48 minutes
3. Scott Lautman, 49, Seattle, Washington, 2 hours, 53 minutes
4. Tim Kulka, 32, Watertown, 3 hours, 17 minutes (tied with Maldonado)
   Victor Maldonado, 38, Watertown, 3 hours, 17 minutes (tied with Kulka)
6. Kate Matwychuk, 31, Middlebury, Vermont, 3 hours, 19 minutes (tied with Knight)
   Fred Knight, 52, Wayland, 3 hours, 19 minutes (tied with Matwychuk)
8. Cecelia Buchanan, 26, Jamaica Plain, 3 hours, 37 minutes
9. Orin McCluskey, 51, New York, New York, 4 hours, 6 minutes

Wetsuits

Ajae Clearway (wetsuit), 31, Brooklyn, New York, 4 hours, 5 minutes

Susan Yeomans,(wetsuit), 53, New York, New York, 4 hours, 13 minutes

Relay Teams

1. Jennifer Dutton, 33, Framingham; Dave Kramer, 28, Jamaica Plain; John Werner, 32, Dorchester, 3 hours, 30 minutes
2. Tom Dugan, 50, Norton; Rob Simms, 47, Cohasset; Joe Carson, 38, Dorchester, 3 hours, 33 minutes

Non-finisher

Fred Schlicher, 52, Medford

Race coordinator, John Werner

2003

The 2003 Boston Light Swim Race was held on August 16. At 9:30 a.m., seven solo swimmers and two relay team members jumped into 62 degree water at the Light. Skies were overcast, wind was moderate from the southwest, and water was a low chop. Beyond the Long Island Bridge, the skies cleared, the water warmed to about 67 degrees, but the chop got worse as the wind moved around to the west, and there was the usual high number of pleasure boats. All swimmers reached the finish at the L Street Beach. Results as follows:

1. Will Riddell, 35, Cambridge, 3 hours, 5 minutes
2. Doug Bosley, 41, Somerville, 3 hours 7 minutes
3. Tommy Kliem, 25, Hong Kong, 3 hours, 24 minutes
4. Mike Kazarnowicz, 25, Allentown, Pennsylvania, 3 hours, 25 minutes
5. Allison Riley, 26, Savannah, Georgia, 3 hours, 41 minutes
6. Victor Maldonado, 39, Watertown, 3 hours, 59 minutes
7. Susan Yeomans, 54, New York, New York, 6 hours, 57 minutes (it deserves special mention that Susan Yeomans made the swim in 2002 in a wetsuit. At age 54, in 2003, she decided to brave the cold water without a wetsuit and finished the swim).

Relay Teams

1. Mike Gates, 46, Groton; Mike Hurley, 46, Ayer, Fred Knight, 53, Wayland, 3 hours, 49 minutes
2. John Werner, 33, Dorchester, George Tlucko, 50, Boxford, 4 hours 10 minutes

Race coordinator, John Werner.

2004

On August 1 at 7:25 a.m., ten solo swimmers and members of three relay teams jumped in at the Light to start the 2004 Boston Light Swim. Water temperature ranged from 62 to 66 degrees. Water from the Light to George's Island had something more than a moderate chop. Then, approaching Rainsford Island, the water settled down to nearly flat. Past Rainsford, the waves kicked up again and the water stayed choppy all the way to Thompson Island. Between Thompson and the finish line, the chop abated somewhat and became more manageable. Nine of the ten soloists, and all of the relay teams, reached the L Street Beach:

1. Bill Ireland, 45, Los Angeles, California, 3 hours, 14 minutes
2. Leonard Jansen, 49, Elizabethtown, Pennsylvania, 3 hours, 40 minutes
3. Doug Belkin, 36, Cambridge, 3 hours, 44 minutes
4. Fred Knight, 54, Wayland, 4 hours, 1 minute
5. Shane Collins, 54, Vancouver, British Columbia, 4 hours, 5 minutes
   Debbie Collins, 44, Vancouver, British Columbia, 4 hours, 5 minutes (tied with Shane)
7. Mutlu Ozdogan, Cambridge (native of Istanbul, Turkey), 4 hours, 18 minutes
8. Clare Payne, 28, Sydney, Australia, 4 hours, 32 minutes
9. Ellen Clay, 45, Atlanta, Georgia, 6 hours, 59 minutes

Non-finisher
Joan Kelley, 53, Framingham

Relay Teams
1. Mike Welsch (Iron Mike), David Potere, Tom Dugan, Boston, 5 hours, 23 minutes
2. Joe Oakes, Gary Emich, San Francisco, California, 5 hours, 38 minutes
3. Norman Davis, Jill Moberg, Steve Hurwitz, San Francisco, California, 5 hours, 38 minutes

Race Coordinator. John Werner

2005

2005's Boston Light Swim got off at 7:30 a.m. on August 6. Water temperature at the start was about 65 degrees, with a slight chop. Eleven solo swimmers, and a member of one relay team, dove in. With the calm conditions, all swimmers finished at L Street. The usual increase in choppiness, and presence of numerous powerboats, occurred after the Long Island Bridge, but ideal conditions continued.

Finishers
1. Dori Miller, 34, Somerville, 3 hours, 4 minutes
2. Roberta Bernet, 39, Wadenswil, Switzerland, 3 hours, 11 minutes

2005 participants
Credit John Werner

3. Doug Belkin, 37, Swampscott, 3 hours, 17 minutes
4. Dave Weisfeldt, Durango, Colorado, 3 hours, 22 minutes
5. Jennifer Dutton, 36, Framingham, 3 hours, 41 minutes
6. Kate Matwychuk, 34, Ontario, Canada, 3 hours, 44 minutes
7. Bill Wilson, 52, Butler, Pennsylvania, 3 hours, 46 minutes
8. Michael Stanton, 49, San Diego, California, 3 hours, 49 minutes
9. Mutlu Ozgodan, 34, Istanbul, Turkey, 3 hours, 52 minutes
10. Robert McCormack, 67, Brockton, 5 hours, 29 minutes

Mark Lautman, 55, (wetsuit), 3 hours, 47 minutes

Relay Team

Celia Knight, Brooklyn, New York, Fred Knight, Wayland, 3 hours, 26 minutes

Robert McCormack (your author), at age 67, became the oldest Boston Light Swim finisher in the history of the swim to date, older by only one year than the previous record-holder, Dr. Selwyn Kanosky, who finished the swim, at age 66, in 1995.

Race coordinator, John Werner.

2006

The start time for 2006's Boston Light Swim was 8:45 a.m. on August 12. The water at the start was approximately 62 degrees, with about a one-foot chop. Seventeen solo swimmers, and members of five relay teams, dove in at the Light. At the Long Island Bridge the water became extremely choppy, with at least two to three-foot waves, head-on. Three solo swimmers were forced out at, or before, this stretch, including your author, who retired abreast of the dock at Spectacle Island. The remaining thirteen solo swimmers, and all of the relay teams, finished at L Street:

Finishers
1. Mark Warkentin, 26, Santa Barbara, California, 2 hours, 26 minutes (third best all time to David Alleva of Quincy's 2 hours, 20 minutes in 1995, and Alleva's 2 hours, 23 minutes in 1996)
2. Craig Lewin, 20, Swampscott, 2 hours, 46 minutes
3. Dori Miller, 35, Arlington, 2 hours, 58 minutes
4. Doug Belkin, 38, Cambridge, 3 hours, 18 minutes
5. Greg O'Connor, 37, Natick, 3 hours, 28 minutes
6. Gil Sharon, 32, Westborough, 3 hours, 35 minutes
7. Elaine Kornbau, 28, Waltham, 3 hours, 37 minutes
8. Vince Herring, Rochester, Minnesota, 3 hours, 51 minutes
9. Tim Kulka, 36, Wellesley, 3 hours, 55 minutes
10. Joe Wolf, Denver, Colorado, 3 hours, 59 minutes
11. Brian Mozinski, Hingham, 4 hours, 7 minutes
12. Anthony Stamp, Jamaica Plain, 5 hours, 1 minute
13. Jessica Weather, Jacksonville, Florida, 5 hours, 6 minutes

Amy Black, 25, Boston (wetsuit), 4 hours, 25 minutes

Relay Teams
1. George Hunihan, Vin Hunihan, Lauren Tully, Milford, Connecticut, 3 hours, 33 minutes
2. Lisa Natkins, Mei-An Tsu, Chestnut Hill, 3 hours, 50 minutes,
3. Shoshanna Enich, Rick Borrin, Ramzi Nasir, Tommy Gastell, Brookline, 3 hours, 56 minutes
4. Steven Puopolo, Dan Racki, Dave Sweeney, Scott Fitzgerald, Groveland, 4 hours, 47 minutes

Wetsuits: Tara Gulla, Tommy Gainer, Jim Defoe, Boston, 3 hours, 20 minutes

Non-finishers
Bob McCormack, 68, Brockton
Larry Weiss, Boston
Matt Weiss, Boston

Race coordinator, John Werner.

2007

On August 18, sixteen solo swimmers and members of three relay teams dove in at Boston Light. Conditions were horrendous, possibly the worst in the modern era. Wind was from the northwest, sustained at 25 miles per hour, gusting up to 44, with waves over nearly the entire course at three to four feet, most head-on. Only at the approach to L Street did the waves abate somewhat, with the protection of the landmass. Water temperature at the start was about 65 degrees, but dropped to about 60 degrees during the race. Eleven soloists and two relay teams (one relay team disqualified because of wearing wetsuits), finished at the L Street Beach:

1. Ray Gandy, 45, Coventry, Rhode Island, 3 hours, 29 minutes
2. Joe Sheehan, 36, Melrose, 3 hours, 30 minutes
3. Mallory Mead, 21, Bowling Green, Kentucky, 3 hours, 35 minutes
4. Sebastian Neumayer, 24, Cambridge, 3 hours, 36 minutes
5. Clara Bennett, 18, Granger, Indiana, 3 hours, 54 minutes
6. Elaine Kornbau, 29, Waltham, 4 hours, 22 minutes
7. Anthony Zamora, 46, Los Angeles, California, 4 hours, 24 minutes
8. George Hunihan, 53, Milford, Connecticut, 4 hours, 39 minutes
9. William Wilson, 54, Butler, Pennsylvania, 5 hours, 12 minutes
10. John Sullivan, 45, Brooklyn, New York, 5 hours, 19 minutes
11. Michael Gemelli, 37, Rutherford, New Jersey, 5 hours, 19 minutes

David Evangelista, 44, Medford (wetsuit), 5 hours, 40 minutes

Relay Teams

Tied: 5 hours, 31 minutes

Steven Puopolo, David Miles, Dan Racki, average age 49, Groveland
David Sweeney, Scott Fitzgerald, Bob Somma, average age 49, Groveland

Wetsuits: Amy Black, 26, Jason Black, 29, Boston, 5 hours, 55 minutes

Non-finishers

Joel Lanz, 34, San Francisco, California
Gil Sharon, 33, Westboro
Kellie Joyce, 21, Cumberland, Maine
Fred Knight, 57, Wayland

Race coordinator, John Werner

2008

Sixteen solo swimmers and a member of one relay team started the 2008 Boston Light Swim at 7 a.m. on August 2. Fourteen of the sixteen soloists, and the relay team finished at the L Street Beach.

Finishers

1. Sebastian Neumayer, 25, Cambridge, 2 hours, 44 minutes
   Ray Gandy, 46, Coventry, Rhode Island, 2 hours, 44 minutes (tied for first place)
3. Michelle Macy, 31, Portland, Oregon, 2 hours, 47 minutes
4. Greg O'Connor, 39, Natick, 2 hours, 54 minutes
5. Gil Sharon, 34, Westborough, 3 hours, 8 minutes
6. Joni Young, 47, Salem, Oregon, 3 hours, 9 minutes

7. Andreas Hilfinger, 31, Jamaica Plain, 3 hours, 17 minutes
8. Elaine Kornbau-Howley, 30, Waltham, 3 hours, 25 minutes
9. Dana Farrell, 33, Washington DC, 3 hours, 26 minutes
10. Eileen Burke, 45, New York, New York, 3 hours, 31 minutes
11. Conor Hartnett, 41, Babylon, New York, 3 hours, 40 minutes
12. Stephen Autry, 60, Cincinnati, Ohio, 3 hours, 48 minutes
13. Francis Fidler, 52, Naples, Florida, 4 hours, 16 minutes
14. Laura Colette, 44, Nahant, 4 hours, 39 minutes

Relay Team

Ali Maglievi, 36, Southborough; Mike Brock, 47, Loveland, Ohio; Devin Brock, 14, South Boston: 3 hours, 34 minutes

Non-finishers

Tara Gulla, 35, Newton

Kiko Bracker, 39, Roslindale

Race coordinator, John Werner

2009

2009's Boston Light Swim had seventeen solo swimmers, and three relay team members take to the water at the Light at 8 a.m., August 8. The water was cold, about 60 degrees at the start, rising to the low to mid-sixties near the finish, the wind at 12 miles per hour from the north/northwest, chop 1 1/2 to 2 feet for the duration of the swim.

Twelve of the seventeen solo swimmers, and all three of the relay teams, finished at L Street:

Finishers
1. Sebastian Neumayer, 26, Cambridge, 2 hours, 57 minutes
2. Andrew McMorrow, 3 hours, 19 minutes
3. Jessica Stokes, 3 hours, 21 minutes
4. Kate Radville, 3 hours, 25 minutes
5. Lauren Tharaud, 3 hours, 38 minutes
6. Charles Mitchell, 3 hours, 39 minutes
7. William Lee, 3 hours, 42 minutes
8. Darren Tedesco, 3 hours, 53 minutes
9. Eileen Burke, 46, Brooklyn, New York, 3 hours, 58 minutes
10. Willy Blumentals, 4 hours, 15 minutes
11. David Evangelista, 46, Medford, 4 hours, 21 minutes
12. Kim Garbarino, 51, Winthrop, 4 hours, 25 minutes

Relay Teams
1. Rick Gaenzle, Chris Kraus: 3 hours, 44 minutes
2. Douglas McKell, Kyle Murray, James Walker: 3 hours, 58 minutes
3. Rebecca Osborn, Amy Wu: 4 hours, 13 minutes

Non-finishers

Kimberly Plewa

Susan Jepsen

Darlene Awalt

John Daprato, 56, Brooklyn, New York

Michael Siry

The new Boston Light Swim Race Committee for 2009: Greg O'Connor, Elaine Kornbau-Howley, and Paula Garland.

2010

The Boston Light Swim of 2010 took place on August 14. Twenty-five solo swimmers started at 7 a.m., along with four relay team members. Water temperature at the Light was 59 degrees.

Finishers
1. Elizabeth Mancuso, 24, Brookline, 2 hours, 42 minutes
2. Dori Miller, 39, Bondi Beach, Australia, 2 hours 42 minutes (30 seconds behind Mancuso)
3. Lance Ogren, 39, New York, New York, 2 hours, 42 minutes (12 seconds behind Miller)
4. Robert Fernald, 43, North Hampton, New Hampshire, 2 hours, 52 minutes
5. Davis Lee, 35, Newburyport, 2 hours, 58 minutes
6. Humphrey Bohan, 35, Medford Lakes, New Jersey, 2 hours, 58 minutes (20 seconds behind Lee)
7. David Barra, 45, High Falls, New York, 3 hours
8. Don MacDonald, 48, Barrington, Illinois, 3 hours, 1 minute
9. Douglas McConnell, 52, Barrington, Illinois, 3 hours, 8 minutes
10. Sheryl Bierden, 37, Westwood, 3 hours, 15 minutes
11. Eileen Burke, 47, Brooklyn, New York, 3 hours, 24 minutes
12. Kyle Murray, 51, Amherst, New Hampshire, 3 hours, 30 minutes
13. Kim Garbarino, 52, Winthrop, 3 hours, 39 minutes
14. Mike Hodel, 33, Somerville, 3 hours, 39 minutes (32 seconds behind Garbarino)
15. Courtney Paulk, 40, Richmond, Virginia, 3 hours, 44 minutes
16. Ralph MacIntyre, 59, Merritt Island, Florida, 3 hours, 47 minutes

17. Alan Morrison, 48, New York, New York, 3 hours, 48 minutes

18. Rachel Golub, 33, Astoria, New York, 3 hours, 48 minutes

19. Dave Evangelista, 47, Medford, 4 hours, 14 minutes

20. John Daprato, 57, Brooklyn New York, 4 hours, 23 minutes

Relay Teams

1. Sebastian Neumayer, Santiago Lima, John Kelleher, 2 hours 42 minutes

2. Doug McKell, James Walker, Bobby Dawe, 3 hours, 36 minutes

3. Mike Ribeiro, Rebecca Osborn, 3 hours, 45 minutes

4. Amy Wu, Silverio Bracaglia, 4 hours, 3 minutes

Non-finishers

Suzanne Sataline, 47, Brooklyn, New York

Kenn Lowy, 53, Brooklyn, New York

Dave Osmond, 63, Wayland

William Dailey, 48, Galveston, Texas

Darlene Awalt, 52, Harwich

Race coordinators, Elaine Kornbau Howley and Greg O'Connor.

On July 27, 2010, Boston Light swimmer, Kim Garbarino, 52, of Winthrop, became only the second person in history to swim a round trip over the eight-mile route, from Boston Light to the South Boston Yacht Club and then back to the Light, a total of 16 miles. He was the first swimmer to accomplish the feat starting at the Light, swimming in to South Boston and returning to the Light. His time for the round-trip was 8 hours, 5 minutes, a new record for the swim. The old record was set by Jim Doty, who did it in 1969 in a time of 9 hours, 12 minutes.

Kim Garbarino's round-trip speed record did not hold for long. On August 12, 2010, Boston Light Swim Race Coordinators, Elaine Kornbau Howley, 32, and Greg O'Connor, 41, swam from South Boston to Boston Light and back, starting and finishing together, in a joint record time of 7 hours, 7 minutes. The pair left the L Street beach at 3:40 a.m., in 62 degree water. By the time they reached the Light, three and a half hours later, the water temperature had dropped to 59 degrees. The return trip took 3 hours, 37 minutes. The water was calm throughout, and fortunately warmed up on the return swim.

2011

On August 13, at about 7 a.m., nineteen solo swimmers and members of five relay teams entered the water at the Boston Light for the 2011 race. Water temperature stayed at about 65 degrees for the duration of the swim, with the winds nearly calm. The sky remained clear, with air temperature in the low to mid-seventies. At the start at Little Brewster Island, there was about a one and a half foot chop. The water became smoother as the swim progressed, but on the Boston side of the Long Island Bridge, the one and a half foot chop returned due to the increase in the number of pleasure boats. Eighteen of the nineteen soloists, and all of the relay teams, finished at L Street as follows:

1. Matthew McKay, 39, Wellesley, 2 hours, 41 minutes
2. Robert Fernald, 43, North Hampton, New Hampshire, 3 hours, 3 minutes
3. Charlotte Brynn, 45, Stowe, Vermont, 3 hours, 6 minutes
4. Paul Goudreau, 45, Lexington, 3 hours, 10 minutes
5. Tommy Gainer, 34, Swampscott, 3 hours, 11 minutes
6. Davis Lee, 36, Newburyport, 3 hours, 12 minutes

Greg O'Connor
Credit Greg O'Connor

Kim Garbarino
Credit Amy Garbarino

Elaine Kornbau-Howley
Credit Mark Howley

7. Anthony McCarley, 52, Berwyn, Pennsylvania, 3 hours, 15 minutes
8. James Brooks, 53, North Falmouth, 3 hours, 26 minutes
9. Michael Phelan, 50, Essex, 3 hours, 31 minutes
10. David Pike, 50, Wellfleet, 3 hours, 33 minutes
11. Eileen Burke, 48, New York, New York, 3 hours, 34 minutes
12. James Walker, 40, Cambridge, 3 hours, 41 minutes
13. Kim Garbarino, 53, Winthrop, 3 hours, 42 minutes
14. Mo Siegel, 59, Piermont, New York, 3 hours, 53 minutes
15. Courtney Paulk, 41, Richmond, Virginia, 4 hours, 11 minutes
16. David Evangelista, 48, Medford, 4 hours, 21 minutes
17. Robert Dawe, 45, Wayland, 4 hours, 23 minutes
18. David Osmond, 64, Wayland, 4 hours, 23 minutes (7 seconds behind Dawe) David Osmond, at 64, became the third oldest Boston Light Swim finisher in history.

Relay teams
1. Sheryl Bierden, Elizabeth Mancuso, B.J. Brannan, Noel LaPierre, 2 hours, 43 minutes
2. Damon Bosetti, Colin Piepgras, Jerome Leslie, 3 hours, 15 minutes
3. Suzanne Sataline, Melissa Kretschmer, 3 hours, 39 minutes
4. John Daprato, Melinda Beck, 4 hours, 9 minutes
5. Rick Sweeney, Francis O'Loughlin, 4 hours, 22 minutes

Non-finisher
Franklin Soukup, 42, Richmond, Virginia

Race coordinators, Elaine Kornbau-Howley and Greg O'Connor.

2012

Twenty-two solo swimmers and seven relay team members dove in at Boston Light on August 18, at 7 a.m. The day was bleak, cloudy and drizzly. Fortunately, the inclement weather kept pleasure craft to a minimum: ferryboats, tugboats and fishing boats were virtually the only vessels on the water. Air and water temperature remained at about 65 degrees for the entire swim. The water was calm, with wave height, for the most part, less than one foot. All twenty-two swimmers and all seven of the relay teams finished at the L Street Beach.

1. Eric Nilsson, 25, Honolulu, Hawaii and Weston, Mass., 2 hours, 35 minutes
2. Andrew Malinak, Brooklyn, New York, 3 hours, 2 minutes
3. Lauren Au, Cambridge, 3 hours, 4 minutes
4. David Swensen, Beverly, 3 hours, 5 minutes
5. Nathaniel Dean, New York, New York, 3 hours, 6 minutes
6. Bob Fernald, 44, North Hampton, New Hampshire, 3 hours, 12 minutes

7. Liz Wong, Groton, Connecticut, 3 hours, 20 minutes
8. Davis Lee, 37, Newburyport, 3 hours, 21 minutes
9. Patricia Flanagan, Boylston, 3 hours, 30 minutes
10. Elias Falcon, Brooklyn, New York, 3 hours, 32 minutes
11. Kenn Lichtenwalter, New York, New York, 3 hours, 36 minutes
12. James J. Feeney, Long Beach, New York, 3 hours, 40 minutes
13. Jennifer Dutton, 43, Wayland, 3 hours, 46 minutes
14. James Walker, 41, Cambridge, 3 hours, 58 minutes
15. Kyle Murray, 53, Amherst, New Hampshire, 4 hours, 6 minutes
16. William Dailey, 50, Galveston, Texas, 4 hours, 8 minutes
17. Kim Garbarino, 54, Winthrop, 4 hours, 12 minutes
18. Laura Colette, Beverly, 4 hours, 21 minutes
19. Richard Sweeney, South Boston, 4 hours, 44 minutes
20. Anita Loughlin, South Boston, 5 hours, 3 minutes
21. Francis O'Loughlin, South Boston, 5 hours, 3 minutes (17 seconds after Loughlin)
22. Douglas McKell, Springfield, 5 hours, 3 minutes (22 seconds after O'Loughlin)

Relay Teams
1. Free Stiles, Reading, 3 hours, 7 minutes
2. NU Harbor Seals, Medford, 3 hours, 12 minutes
3. Stiles Pond Scummers, Andover, 3 hours, 13 minutes
4. Knuckleheads, 3 hours, 14 minutes
5. SOS, Kingston, Rhode Island, 3 hours, 34 minutes
6. Chill Factor, Brooklyn, New York, 4 hours, 1 minute
7. A Team to be Named Later, Wayland, 4 hours, 26 minutes

Race coordinators, Greg O'Connor and Elaine Kornbau-Howley

On April 17, 2012, marathon and Boston Light swimming legend, Jim Doty, passed away at the age of seventy-five. Ocean swimmers, especially in the Boston area, had lost a great advocate, a friend and mentor who can never be replaced, and will never be forgotten. Jim was inducted into the International Marathon Swimming Hall of Fame in 2002.

On August 12, 54-year-old Kim Garbarino, swam from England to France, across the English Channel, in a time of 15 hours, 37 minutes. Amazingly, only six days later he successfully finished the Boston Light Swim Race.

On August 16, three Boston Light swimmers completed the arduous 20 mile swim from White Horse Beach, Plymouth, across Cape Cod Bay to the tip of the Cape, Provincetown. Boston Light race coordinator, and finisher in 2006 and 2008, Greg O'Connor, 43, Boston, Eileen Burke, 49, New York and Orleans, Massachusetts, Boston Light finisher in 2008, 2009, 2010 and 2011, and David Barra, 45, High Falls, New York, Boston Light finisher in 2010, entered the water in the early morning. Also making the attempt that day were New York area residents, Janet Harris, 46, and Mo Siegel, 60. In spite of several prior attempts by other swimmers, only one, Russell Chaffee, 41, of Sayre, Pennsylvania, was ever able to complete the swim, in 1968, in 14 hours, 40 minutes. O'Connor walked up on the Provincetown shore after a swim of 10 hours, 30 minutes, Burke in 11 hours, 10 minutes, Barra and Harris in 11 hours, 55 minutes. (Mo Siegel was forced to retire with an injury but did succeed in the crossing, at age 61, in 2013).

2013

At 9 a.m., on August 10, twenty-two solo swimmers and six relay team members jumped into the water at Boston Light for 2013's eight mile race to the L Street Beach. The day started with sunny skies, light winds and a mild chop in 62 degree water. Before most of the swimmers could reach L Street, however, the wind picked up, with a resulting high, head-on chop. The rough conditions, and five hour time limit, prevented ten of the twenty-two soloists, and one of the six relay teams, from finishing. It appeared that several of the unsuccessful swimmers could have reached the beach at L Street if they had more time. Many of these swimmers were held up by the choppy, windy conditions on the last stretch, between Thompson Island and L Street and could not make it in under the five hour time limit.

Finishers
1. Eric Nilsson, 26, Honolulu, Hawaii and Weston, Mass., 2 hours, 45 minutes
2. Rob Jones, 48, Charlottesville, Virginia, 3 hours, 2 minutes
3. Richard McKern, Summit, New Jersey, 3 hours, 9 minutes
4. Allyson Parent, 27, Tewksbury, 3 hours, 18 minutes
5. Andrew Jones, 41, Swampscott, 3 hours, 18 minutes (25 seconds behind Parent)
6. Zachary Cordero, 3 hours, 21 minutes
7. Bob Burrow, Weston, 3 hours, 49 minutes
8. Elias Falcon, Brooklyn, NY, 3 hours, 59 minutes
9. Kim Garbarino, 55, Winthrop, 4 hours, 8 minutes
10. Jonathan Gladstone, 43, 4 hours, 15 minutes
11. Devon Dear, Somerville, 4 hours, 20 minutes
12. James Haynes, 37, North Shore of Massachusetts, 4 hours, 50 minutes

Non-finishers
Courtney Paulk, 43, Richmond, Virginia
Richard Sweeney

Sylvia Marino

Tom Currier

David Kilroy

Francis O'Loughlin, South Boston

Don Debaker

Lynne Mulkerrin

Maura Twomey

Jia Jung

Relay Teams
1. Team Trident: Bill Geary, Katie O'Dair, 3 hours, 32 minutes
2. Tuff Competitor: Kari Kastango, Stephen Gillis, Peter Gillis, 4 hours, 1 minute
3. Sibling Rivalry: Nicole Glazer, Benjamin Glazer, 4 hours, 2 minutes
4. Coney Island Stowaways: David Cook, Silverio Bracaglia, John Daprato, 4 hours, 24 minutes
5. SOS: Michael Garr, Brian Gardner, Donald Sorterup, Jon Cooper, 4 hours, 39 minutes

Non-finishers
Boston Cods: Anita Loughlin, Giulia Norton, Wendy McDanolds, Margie Shaughnessy

Race coordinators: Greg O'Connor and Elaine Kornbau-Howley

2014

2014's Boston Light Swim Race got underway on July 26, when 23 solo swimmers and members of six relay teams entered the water at the Light at 7 a.m. Water was about 60 degrees, with a one foot chop at the start, under partly cloudy skies. Between George's Island and the Long Island Bridge, the chop picked up to about two feet, with substantial crosscurrents. Water stayed at about 60 degrees throughout the swim. The choppy conditions continued to the northeast tip of Thompson Island but abated somewhat between that point and the finish at L Street beach. Twenty-one of the 23 solos, and all six of the relay teams finished at L Street.

Finishers
1. Bill Shipp, 54, Mitchellville, Maryland, 2 hours, 59 minutes
2. Nathaniel Dean, 37, New York, N.Y., 3 hours, 8 minutes
3. Elizabeth Fry, 55, Westport, Connecticut, 3 hours, 13 minutes
4. Susan Knight, 46, Kennebunk, Maine, 3 hours, 15 minutes
5. Martin McMahon, 46, Simsbury, Connecticut, 3 hours, 23 minutes
6. Loren King, Hamilton, Ontario, 3 hours, 28 minues
7. John Shumadine, 46, Portland, Maine, 3 hours, 31 minutes
8. Alison Meehan, 43, Elkton, Maryland, 3 hours, 37 minutes

9. Jason Glass, Brookline, 3 hours, 41 minutes
10. Kim Garbarino, 56, Winthrop, 3 hours, 46 minutes
11. Helen Lin, 30, Quincy, 3 hours, 50 minutes,
12. Bryce Croll, 29, Boston, 3 hours, 50 minutes (14 seconds after Lin)
13. Solly Weiler, Newton, 3 hours, 54 minutes
14. Rebecca Burns, New York, N.Y., 3 hours, 56 minutes
15. Kellie Joyce, Norwood, 3 hours, 59 minutes
16. David Conners, San Francisco, California, 4 hours, 3 minutes
17. Courtney Paulk, Richmond, Virginia, 4 hours, 26 minutes
18. David Cook, New York, N.Y., 4 hours, 32 minutes
19. Mo Siegel, Piermont, N.Y., 4 hours, 34 minutes
20. David Kilroy, Marblehead, 4 hours, 46 minutes
21. Jerome Leslie, Dorchester, 4 hours, 53 minutes

Relay Teams
1. Frozen Nipples, Massachusetts, 3 hours, 13 minutes
2. Maine Masters, Maine, 3 hours, 25 minutes
3. Swim4fun, Massachusetts, 3 hours, 32 minutes
4. Tuff Competitor II, Massachusetts, 3 hours, 52 minutes
5. Sachuest Ocean Swimmers, Rhode Island, 3 hours, 59 minutes
6. A Fin & A Prayer, Massachusetts, 4 hours, 40 minutes

Non-finishers
Melissa Hoffman, Sugar Land, Texas
Francis O'Loughlin, South Boston

Dr. Marcy MacDonald, 50, of Andover, CT, three-time finisher, and two-time winner, of the Boston Light Swim Race, swam across the English Channel on June 30. This marked the fifteenth successful channel swim for Marcy, a new record for the most successful crossings of the channel by an American. The previous record-holder was Peter Jurzynski, also a Boston Light swimmer, formerly of South Boston, now living in Naugatuck, Connecticut. Marcy has had a brilliant marathon-swimming career, including three double-crossings of the English Channel. She was inducted into the International Marathon Swimming Hall of Fame in 2005. Marcy vows that there are more great swims in her future, and who would doubt her?

Special Tributes

Note: Swimmers in this section are recognized only for prominence in Boston Light swims and, where applicable, successful English Channel crossings. Several of these athletes also succeeded in other outstanding swims, such as the Strait of Gibraltar, Catalina Island, Lake Winnipesaukee, Graves Light and Cape Ann. These accomplishments, certainly extraordinary and important, are too numerous to mention here. All of the Boston Light swims are eight miles except where otherwise noted.

David Alleva

| 1995 | 41 | First place | 2 hours, 20 minutes | fastest Boston Light swim of all time |
| 1996 | 42 | First place | 2 hours, 23 minutes | second fastest all time |

One of only four swimmers to finish the Boston Light Swim twice in less than three hours. He only swam Boston Light twice.

Sharon Beckman

1981	23	Second place	2 hours, 51 minutes (6-miles)
1982	24	First place	3 hours, 7 minutes
1982		English Channel in 9 hours, 7 minutes, becoming the first New England woman to accomplish the feat.

Doug Belkin

2004	36	Third place	3 hours, 44 minutes
2005	37	Third place	3 hours, 17 minutes
2006	38	Fourth place	3 hours, 18 minutes

Margaret Broenniman

| 1983 | 20 | First place | 3 hours, 27 minutes |
| 1984 | 21 | English Channel | 11 hours, 30 minutes |

Eileen Burke

1998	35	Fourth place	3 hours, 49 minutes
2008	45	Tenth place	3 hours, 31 minutes
2009	46	Ninth place	3 hours, 58 minutes
2010	47	Eleventh place	3 hours, 24 minutes
2011	48	Eleventh place	3 hours, 34 minutes

Julie Burnett

1993	27	First place	3 hours, 41 minutes
1994	28	First place	3 hours, 38 minutes
2000	34	Sixth place	4 hours, 33 minutes

Marcia Cleveland

2002	38	First place	2 hours, 47 minutes
1994	30	English Channel	

James J. Doty

1976	39	First place	5 hours, 39 minutes-11 miles
1977	40	Third place	5 hours, 29 minutes-11 miles
1978	41	Third place	5 hours, 34 minutes-11 miles
1980	43	Third place	4 hours, 45 minutes-9 miles
1981	44	Sixth place	3 hours, 43 minutes-6 miles
1982	45	Seventh place	4 hours, 9 minutes *this and all remaining swims 8 miles*
1983	46	Eighth place	4 hours, 32 minutes
1984	47	Third place	5 hours, 15 minutes
1985	48	Seventh place	4 hours, 32 minutes
1986	49	Did not finish-ulcer attack	
1987	50-	Sixth place	4 hours, 12 minutes
1988	51	Fourth place	4 hours, 33 minutes
1989	52	Fifth place	4 hours, 47 minutes
1990	53-	Fifth place	5 hours, 39 minutes
1968	31	Solo Boston Light swim	4 hours, 32 minutes
1969	32	2-way Boston Light swim	9 hours, 12 minutes

1992, 1993, 1994, 1995, 1998, 1999   Boston Light relay swims

First swimmer of the Boston Light in 27 years

First to successfully complete a 2-way swim over the 8-mile route

Record holder for the most successful Boston Light Swims: 16 of 17 attempts

Record holder for the most successful Boston Light solo and relay swims combined: 22

Tom Dugan

1995	44	Sixth place	3 hours, 28 minutes
1996	45	Sixth place	3 hours, 14 minutes
1998	47	Fifth place	4 hours, 4 minutes
1999	48	First place	4 hours, 36 minutes

Jennifer Dutton

1996	27	Fifth place	3 hours, 2 minutes
1998	29	Third place	3 hours, 43 minutes
1999	30	Fourth place	time not recorded
2001	32	Fourth place	6 hours, 7 minutes
2005	36	Fifth place	3 hours, 41 minutes
2012	43	Thirteenth place	3 hours, 46 minutes

David Evangelista

2009	46	Eleventh place	4 hours, 21 minutes
2010	47	Ninetenth place	4 hours, 14 minutes
2011	48	Sixteenth place	4 hours, 21 minutes

Maura Fitzpatrick

1980	16	Second place	4 hours, 35 minutes (9 miles)
1983	19	Second place	3 hours, 43 minutes
1984	20	English Channel	11 hours, 30 minutes.

Ray Gandy

2007	45	First place	3 hours, 29 minutes
2008	46	First place (tied with Sebastian Neumayer)	2 hours, 44 minutes

Kim Garbarino

Only person to have successfully completed three 2-way swims over the 8-mile course.

2009	51	Twelfth place	4 hours, 25 minutes
2010	52	Thirteenth place	3 hours, 39 minutes
2011	53	Thirteenth place	3 hours, 42 minutes
2012	54	Seventeenth place	4 hours 12 minutes
2013	55	Ninth place	4 hours, 8 minutes
2014	56	Tenth place	3 hours, 46 minutes
2010	52	2-way	8 hours, 5 minutes (new record)
2012	54	English Channel	15 hours, 37 minutes
2013	55	2-way	7 hours, 24 minutes
2014	56	2-way	8 hours, 23 minutes
2014	56	Swam the old 12-mile Boston Light Swim course (first person since 1938) 4 hours, 34 minutes (second fastest time ever)

Second highest number of successful Boston Light swims: 13

Brian Hanley

1978	28	First place	4 hours, 51 minutes (11 miles)
1980	30	First place	4 hours, 10 minutes (9 miles)
1982	32	Fouth place	3 hours, 30 minutes

Karen Hartley

1981	24	Third place	3 hours, 10 minutes (6-miles)
1982	25	Third place	3 hours, 19 minutes
1986	29	Fourth place	5 hours, 33 minutes
1987	30	Fourth place	3 hours, 42 minutes

Elaine Kornbau-Howley

2006	28	Seventh place	3 hours, 37 minutes
2007	29	Sixth place	4 hours, 22 minutes
2008	30	Eighth place	3 hours 25 minutes
2010	32	2-way	7 hours, 7 minutes (co-holder of record fastest time ever)
2009	31	English Channel	13 hours, 35 minutes

Peter Jurzynski

1980	29	Fourth place	4 hours, 57 minutes (9 miles)
1983	32	Fourth place	3 hours, 52 minutes
1984	33	Second place	4 hours, 17 minutes
1985	34	Fourth place	3 hours, 40 minutes
1986	35	Third place	4 hours, 30 minutes
1987	36	Third place	3 hours, 35 minutes
1988	37	Second place	4 hours, 21 minutes

Held the record for most successful English Channel crossings by an American (until 2014), with fourteen between 1987 and 2007 (see page 15 for English Channel record).

Dr. Selwyn Kanosky

1995	66	Ninth place	5 hours, 45 minutes

Oldest finisher of the Boston Light Swim until 2005, currently second oldest ever (as of 2014).

Fred Knight

2000	50	Fourth place	3 hours, 58 minutes
2001	51	First place	4 hours, 59 minutes
2002	52	Sixth place	3 hours, 19 minutes
2004	54	Fourth place	4 hours, 1 minute

John Langton
1996	29	Fourth place	2 hours, 58 minutes
1998	31	Second place	3 hours, 24 minutes
2000	33	Sixth place	4 hours, 33 minutes

Davis Lee
2010	35	Fifth place	2 hours, 58 minutes
2011	36	Sixth place	3 hours, 12 minutes
2012	37	Eighth place	3 hours, 21 minutes

Dr. Marcy MacDonald
1986	22	First place	4 hours, 4 minutes
1987	23	First place	2 hours, 55 minutes (7-miles)
1995	31	Fourth place	2 hours, 59 minutes

Holds the record for the most successful English Channel swims by an American, completing her fifteenth, at age 50, on June 30, 2014. Her English Channel swims spanned the years 1994 to 2014. They include three double-crossings.

George MacMasters
1989	32	Third place	3 hours, 41 minutes
1991	34	Second place	3 hours, 55 minutes
1992	35	Second place	3 hours, 19 minutes
1994	37	English Channel	12 hours, 10 minutes.

Robert McCormack
1977	39	Did not finish	Made it to Long Island Bridge - 4 miles
2005	67	Tenth place	5 hours, 29 minutes
2006	68	Did not finish	Made it to Spectacle Island - 5 1/2 miles

Oldest swimmer ever to finish the Boston Light Swim as of 2014

Dori Miller
2005	34	First place	3 hours, 4 minutes
2006	35	Third place	2 hours, 58 minutes
2010	39	Second place	2 hours, 42 minutes

One of only four swimmers ever to finish the Boston Light Swim twice in less than three hours. Has made five crossings of the English Channel, including a two-way on August 4, 2014, in a time of 26 hours, 21 minutes.

Sebastian Neumayer

2007	24	Fourth place	3 hours, 36 minutes
2008	25	First place	2 hours, 44 minutes
2009	26	First place	2 hours, 57 minutes

One of only four swimmers ever to finish the Boston Light Swim twice in less than three hours.

Eric Nilsson

| 2012 | 25 | First place | 2 hours, 35 minutes |
| 2013 | 26 | First place | 2 hours, 45 minutes |

One of only four swimmers ever to finish the Boston Light Swim twice in less than three hours.

Greg O'Connor

2006	37	Fifth place	3 hours, 28 minutes
2008	39	Fourth place	2 hours, 54 minutes
2010	41	2-way Boston Light	7 hours, 7 minutes; co-holder of record fastest time

David Osmond

| 2011 | 64 | Eighteenth place | 4 hours, 23 minutes |

Third-oldest swimmer to ever finish the Boston Light Swim

Courtney Paulk:

2010	40	Fifteenth place	3 hours 44 minutes
2011	41	Fifteenth place	4 hours 11 minutes
2013	43	Did not finish	
2014	44	Seventeenth place	4 hours 26 minutes

Jim Peters

| 1989 | | First place | 3 hours, 17 minutes |
| 1990 | | First place | 3 hours, 30 minutes |

Richard Puopolo

1989		Fourth place	4 hours, 43 minutes
1990		Third place	4 hours, 49 minutes
1991		Third place	4 hours, 5 minutes

Jeff Sheard

1983	32	Third place	3 hours, 51 minutes
1984	33	First place	3 hours, 41 minutes
1985	34	Second place	3 hours, 9 minutes
1986	35	Second place	4 hours, 11 minutes
1986	35	English Channel	11 hours, 8 minutes

Mark Warkentin

| 2006 | 26 | First place | 2 hours, 26 minutes; third fastest of all time |

Mike "Iron Mike" Welsch

1992	33	Third place	5 hours, 38 minutes
1993	34	Third place	4 hours, 27 minutes
1994	35	Fourth place	4 hours, 51 minutes
1995	36	Seventh place	3 hours, 34 minutes
2001	42	Fifth place	7 hours, 28 minutes

Mike succeeded in all five swims despite having suffered the loss of a leg in a motorcycle accident at age 20.

John Werner

1998	28	Sixth place	4 hours, 32 minutes
1999	29	Second place	4 hours, 57 minutes
2000	30	Ninth place	5 hours, 44 minutes
2001	31	Second place	5 hours, 55 minutes (in concurrent 6-mile race)

Sub-3-hour Swimmers of the 8-mile Boston Light Course

Only 26 swimmers have swum the 8-mile course in under three hours. Four swimmers, David Alleva, Eric Nilsson, Dori Miller and Sebastian Neumayer, have done it twice. The first person to ever swim the eight mile course in under three hours was Billy Nolan in 1940. Nolan held the record of 2 hours, 46 minutes until it was broken by David Alleva of Quincy, Mass. in 1995, in 2 hours, 20 minutes. His record still stands as of 2014. He also holds the runner-up record of 2 hours, 23 minutes, set in 1996.

The complete list of sub-three hour swimmers is as follows:

David Alleva, 41, Quincy	1995	2 hours, 20 minutes
David Alleva, 42, Quincy	1996	2 hours, 23 minutes
Mark Warkentin, 26, Santa Barbara, California	2006	2 hours, 26 minutes
Eric Nilsson, 25, Honolulu, Hawaii and Weston	2012	2 hours, 35 minutes
John O'Connell, Quincy	1996	2 hours, 40 minutes
Matthew McKay, 39, Wellesley	2011	2 hours, 41 minutes
Elizabeth Mancuso, 24, Brookline	2010	2 hours, 42 minutes
Dori Miller, 39, Bondi Beach, Australia	2010	2 hours, 42 minutes
Lance Ogren, 39, New York, New York	2010	2 hours, 42 minutes
Sebastian Neumayer, 25, Cambridge	2008	2 hours, 44 minutes

Ray Gandy, 46, Coventry, Rhode Island	2008	2 hours, 44 minutes
Eric Nilsson, 26, Honolulu, Hawaii and Weston	2013	2 hours, 45 minutes
Billy Nolan, 26, Charlestown	1940	2 hours, 46 minutes
Craig Lewin, 20, Swampscott	2006	2 hours, 46 minutes
Marcia Cleveland 38, Riverside, Connecticut	2002	2 hours, 47 minutes
Michelle Macy, 31, Portland, Oregon	2008	2 hours, 47 minutes
Nicholas Sidelnik, 20, Overland Park, Kansas	2002	2 hours, 48 minutes
Kasim Kazbay, 32, New York, New York	1995	2 hours, 49 minutes
Art Lutschaunig, Boston	1995	2 hours, 50 minutes
Robert Fernald, 43, North Hampton, New Hampshire	2010	2 hours, 52 minutes
Scott Lautman, 49, Seattle, Washington	2002	2 hours, 53 minutes
Kathleen Hines, New York, New York	1996	2 hours, 54 minutes
Greg O'Connor, 39, Natick	2008	2 hours, 54 minutes
Sebastian Neumayer, 26, Cambridge	2009	2 hours, 57 minutes
John Langton, 29, Woburn	1996	2 hours, 58 minutes
Dori Miller, 35, Arlington	2006	2 hours, 58 minutes
Davis Lee, 35, Newburyport	2010	2 hours, 58 minutes
Humphrey Bohan, 35, Medford, Lakes, New Jersey	2010	2 hours, 58 minutes
Marcy MacDonald, 31, Andover, Connecticut	1995	2 hours, 59 minutes
Bill Shipp, 54, Mitchellville, Maryland	2014	2 hours, 59 minutes

Two-way Swimmers

Elaine Kornbau-Howley	2010	7 hours, 7 minutes
Greg O'Connor	2010	7 hours, 7 minutes
Kim Garbarino	2013	7 hours, 24 minutes
Kim Garbarino	2010	8 hours, 5 minutes
Kim Garbarino	2014	8 hours, 23 minutes
Jim Doty	1969	9 hours, 12 minutes

Kim Garbarino

Kim Garbarino of Winthrop, Massachusetts is the consummate Boston Light swimmer. After participating in only one previous ocean swim race, 2.5 miles in 2008, he entered the Boston Light

Swim Race of 2009, at the age of 51. During that and the following five years, he succeeded in finishing 13 Boston Light swims, including three 2-way swims and one swim over the old 12-mile route, from Charlestown Bridge to the Boston Light. In addition to Boston Light swims, Kim found time to train for and complete an English Channel crossing in 2012, at age 54, in a time of 15 hours, 37 minutes. Now, at age 56, he vows that there are more remarkable swims in his future.

Race Coordinators-1976-2014

Substantial interest in the Boston Light Swim Race did not really occur within the first five years or so of its reorganization in 1976. Significantly, however, interest and involvement in the Race have increased since the early 1980s, and this trend continued under the leadership of John Werner, from 1999 to 2008, and Greg O'Connor and Elaine Kornbau-Howley, from 2009 to the present (2014). Under their capable leadership, the swim promises to remain a strong tradition for the foreseeable future.

Jim Doty: 1976 to 1995

Jim could well be named King of the Boston Light Swim. He reorganized the race in 1976, after a 35-year interruption. During his nineteen years as race coordinator, he participated as a solo swimmer for fourteen straight years, failing to finish only once, due to an ulcer attack in 1986. In addition, he swam six successful relays between 1992 and 1999. Prior to the reorganization of the swim in 1976, Jim "swam the Light" once in 1968, and then succeeded in a non-stop round trip in 1969, finishing in 9 hours, 12 minutes. He established the New England Marathon Swimming Association (NEMSA) in 1978. The Boston Light Swim Race was under that organization's auspices for the rest of Jim's tenure and for many years thereafter.

Andy Frackiewicz: 1996 and 1998

Andy was willing to step in as race coordinator after Jim Doty's retirement in 1995. A qualified replacement had to be found quickly and Andy came forward. He guided the Boston Light Swim Race through this critical time, when the swim's very survival could well have been in jeopardy.

John Werner: 1999 to 2008

John managed to fit in four solo and two relay Boston Light Swims during his incumbency as race coordinator. During his tenure, interest in the Swim remained high, and participation grew steadily.

Fred Knight assisted John for most of his ten years as race coordinator. During this time, Fred not only worked hard as a volunteer but also participated in five Boston Light solo swims, finishing four, winning in 2001. He also swam in, and finished, two Boston Light Swim relays.

Greg O'Connor and Elaine Kornbau-Howley: 2009 to present

Elaine has swum three Boston Light races, in 2006, 2007 and 2008; and one two-way swim in 2010. She and Greg O'Connor swam together in a two-way swim, in 2010, and set a joint speed record of 7 hours, 7 minutes. In addition to his two-way swim, Greg has succeeded in two other Boston Light Swims, in 2006 and 2008. Both Greg and Elaine have also finished many other great marathon swims, and are doing an outstanding job as Boston Light Swim Race coordinators.

About the Author

Robert L. McCormack was born in Brooklyn, New York on November 11, 1937. At the age of seven he moved with his family to the Dorchester section of Boston, Massachusetts. He grew up there and learned to swim at nearby Tenean Beach.

He participated in several ocean swims between the ages of 26 and 41, at which time he retired from ocean swimming to work full time to support his wife and three daughters.

At the age of 64, in 2002, Bob resumed his ocean swimming career, participating in some 50 ocean swims from that date to the present.

Among his successful swims are:

- Boston Light Swim, Boston (8 miles)
  This swim is recorded in the International Marathon Swimming Hall of Fame. Bob became the oldest swimmer, at 67, in 2005, to ever finish the Boston Light Swim.

- 3 times Little Red Lighthouse Swim, Hudson River, New York City (6 miles)

- Governors Island, New York City (2 miles)

- 4 times Alcatraz, San Francisco (1.5 miles)

- Golden Gate Bridge, San Francisco (1.5 miles)

Other books by the author:

- *Alone on a Wide Wide Sea* An account of six of the author's most challenging ocean swims

- *So You Want to Swim Alcatraz* Tips on swimming from Alcatraz to San Francisco by the author, a 4-time successful Alcatraz swimmer

- *The Jim Doty Story* Accounts of some of the marathon swims of a great Boston ocean swimmer

- *Swimming the Light: A Brief History of the Boston Light Swim from 1907 to 1941*

- *Remember the Brave New England's 26th (Yankee) Division with the American Expeditionary Force in WW I France-1917-1919*

www.robertmccormack.com

Made in the USA
Lexington, KY
28 July 2015